Hungry Plants

Lisa J. Amstutz

rourkeeducationalmedia.com

BEFORE AND DURING READING ACTIVITIES

Before Reading: *Building Background Knowledge and Vocabulary*

Building background knowledge can help children process new information and build upon what they already know. Before reading a book, it is important to tap into what children already know about the topic. This will help them develop their vocabulary and increase their reading comprehension.

Questions and Activities to Build Background Knowledge:

1. Look at the front cover of the book and read the title. What do you think this book will be about?
2. What do you already know about this topic?
3. Take a book walk and skim the pages. Look at the table of contents, photographs, captions, and bold words. Did these text features give you any information or predictions about what you will read in this book?

Vocabulary: *Vocabulary Is Key to Reading Comprehension*

Use the following directions to prompt a conversation about each word.
- Read the vocabulary words.
- What comes to mind when you see each word?
- What do you think each word means?

> **Vocabulary Words:**
> - *energy*
> - *minerals*
> - *prey*
> - *tubes*

During Reading: *Reading for Meaning and Understanding*

To achieve deep comprehension of a book, children are encouraged to use close reading strategies. During reading, it is important to have children stop and make connections. These connections result in deeper analysis and understanding of a book.

Close Reading a Text

During reading, have children stop and talk about the following:
- Any confusing parts
- Any unknown words
- Text to text, text to self, text to world connections
- The main idea in each chapter or heading

Encourage children to use context clues to determine the meaning of any unknown words. These strategies will help children learn to analyze the text more thoroughly as they read.

When you are finished reading this book, turn to the last page for an **After Reading Activity**.

Table of Contents

Plants Eat Too

Plants need food to live and grow.

But plants can't chew! So, what do they do?

Plants Make Food

Plants make their own food!

They need light, water, and air. They get **minerals** from soil.

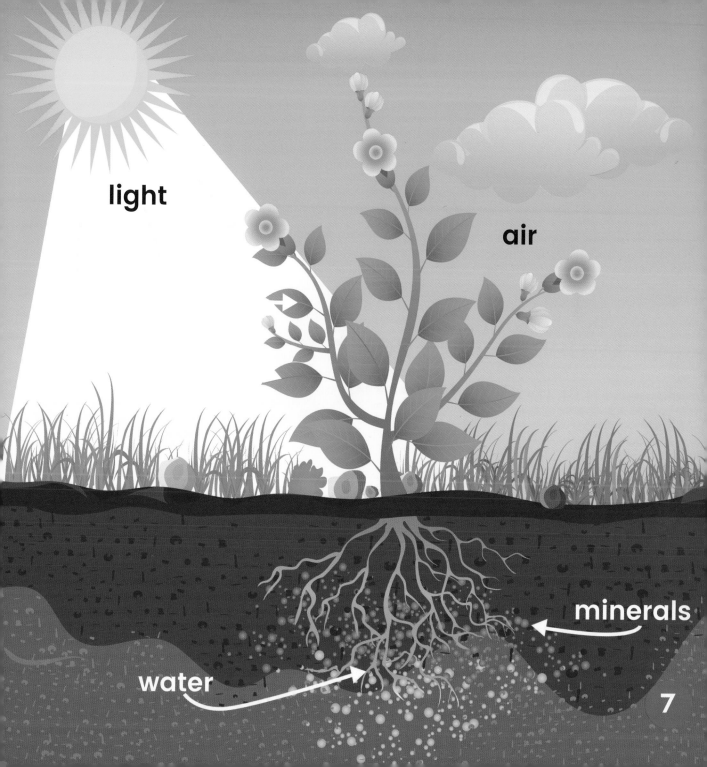

light

air

minerals

water

7

Green leaves catch light. They turn it into **energy**.

Look! A leaf has tiny holes. Air goes in and out.

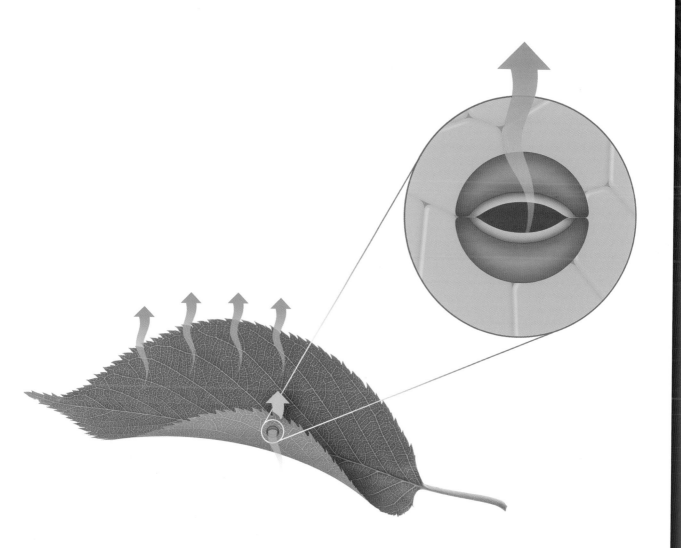

Roots soak up water. Slurp!

Tubes take it to the leaves. They act like straws.

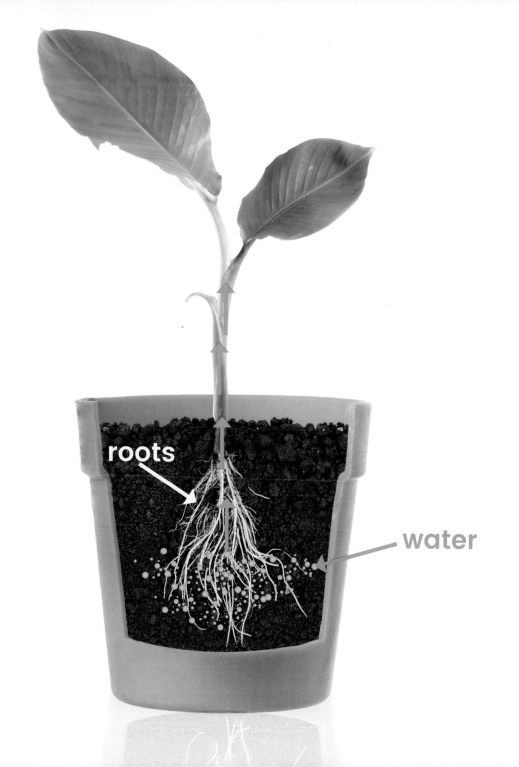

roots

water

13

The air, water, and light mix. This makes sugar!

Sugar is food for plants.

Plants use sugar to grow. They store some too.

Plants Catch Food

Munch! A few plants eat meat. They live in poor soil.

pitcher plant

19

Snap! Leaves can form a trap.

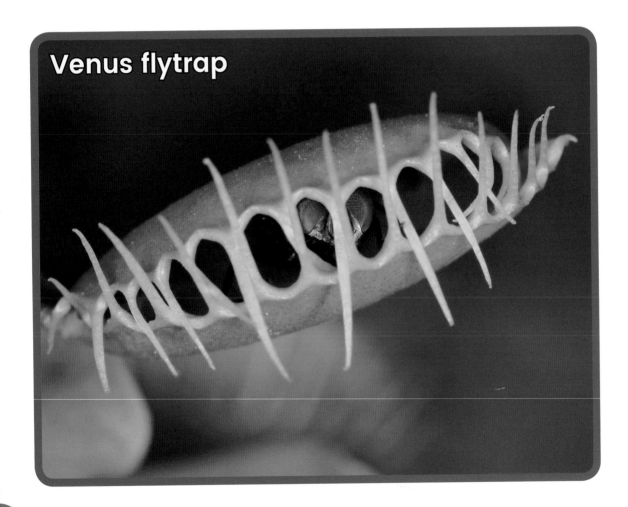

Venus flytrap

Other plants suck in **prey**.
Goodbye, bug!

bladderwort

Photo Glossary

energy (EN-ur-jee): The power needed to do work.

zinc

minerals (MIN-ur-uhls): Solid substances found on Earth that do not come from animals or plants. Plants need minerals such as zinc to grow.

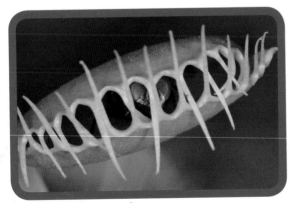

prey (pray): An animal that is hunted for food.

tube

tubes (toobs): Long, hollow cylinders used to carry or hold liquids.

22

Light and Dark

What happens if a plant can't find light?
Let's find out!

Supplies

two small pots

six bean seeds

potting soil

water

Directions

1. Fill each pot with potting soil.
2. Plant three bean seeds in each pot.
3. Water the seeds well.
4. Place one pot in a sunny spot. Place the other pot in a dark room.
5. Water as needed to keep the soil damp.
6. Every few days, compare the plants. Do they look the same? Why or why not?

Index

About the Author

Lisa Amstutz is the author of more than 100 children's books. She loves learning about science and sharing fun facts with kids. Lisa lives on a small farm with her family, two goats, a flock of chickens, and a dog named Daisy.

After Reading Activity

Go outdoors and find a spot where a plant might like to grow. Stretch out your arms. Can you feel the sun? Take a deep breath. Is the air fresh and clean? Look up at the sky. Will rain fall on the plant? If you've found a good spot, try planting a seed!

Library of Congress PCN Data

Hungry Plants / Lisa J. Amstutz
(My Life Science Library)
ISBN 978-1-73161-502-2 (hard cover)(alk. paper)
ISBN 978-1-73161-309-7 (soft cover)
ISBN 978-1-73161-607-4 (e-Book)
ISBN 978-1-73161-712-5 (e-Pub)
Library of Congress Control Number: 2019932045

Rourke Educational Media
Printed in the United States of America,
North Mankato, Minnesota

© 2020 Rourke Educational Media

www.rourkeeducationalmedia.com

Edited by: Kim Thompson
Produced by Blue Door Education for Rourke Educational Media.
Cover and interior design by: Nicola Stratford
Photo Credits: Cover photo © Smileus, fly © denisik11, flytrap © Usenko Oleksandr; pages 4-5 © AVANGARD Photography; page 7 © snapgalleria; pages 8-9 © Triff; page 10 © Aldona Griskeviciene; page 13 © showcake; page 16-17 luck luckyfarm; page 19 © By chockdee Romkaew; page 20 © Marco Uliana, page 21 © Mps197; glossary, image of zinc © KrimKate All images from Shutterstock.com